Now And Then Disciples

By Merlin L. Conrad

C.S.S. Publishing Company, Inc.
Lima, Ohio

NOW AND THEN DISCIPLES

Copyright © 1991 by
The C.S.S. Publishing Company, Inc.
Lima, Ohio

Library of Congress Cataloging-in-Publication Data
Conrad, Merlin L., 1936-
  Now and then disciples / by Merlin L. Conrad
      p.   cm.
  Includes indexes.
ISBN 1-55673-280-5
    1. Lenten sermons.   2. Sermons, American.   3. Apostles—Sermons.
4. Biographical preaching.   I. Title
BV4277.C57   1991
252'.62—dc20   90-42347
                                                                          CIP

9113 / ISBN 1-55673-280-5   PRINTED IN U.S.A.

Dedication

To my father Winfield Scott Conrad, 1889-1971,
from whom I first learned what it means
to be a disciple
and to my children, Scott, Annette and Julia,
inheritors of my faith.

TABLE OF CONTENTS

INTRODUCTION

Each of the Wednesday evening services were set in the mode of a worship context. In every case the Scripture used was that which dealt with the particular Apostle that was to be interviewed. At the normal point of the sermon the Apostles would arrive in first-century garb from the back of the church, making their way to the chancel area, where they would be interviewed in a kind of "You Were There" format.

SCRIPTURE LESSONS

Matthew 4:18-22; 17:13; 20-23 John 13:21-23	James and John
John 18:1-25 Matthew 27:1-5	Peter, Judas
John 6:5-7; 14:8-9; 20:19-29	Philip, Thomas
Acts 1:12-14 Matthew 9:9-13 John 14:22-24	Simon the Zealot, Matthew, Thaddaeus
Matthew 10:1-5 John 1:40, 42; 45-50; 6:8-11	Andrew, Bartholomew, James, son of Alphaeus

FOREWORD

In casual gatherings of experienced clergy the question usually surfaces in mood if not in words, "How do you tell the same story over and over, yet always with freshness and vitality?" Advent, Christmas, Lent, Holy Week, Good Friday, Easter — they come around with predictable regularity. Dr. Conrad, in this series has provided an answer to this question for the Lenten season. In the novel setting of a twentieth-century posthumous interview of those who walked with Jesus and remembered, it examines not only their memories but what the traditions of history have done with them and their memories. Dr. Conrad has done extensive research in drawing together scriptural references, church traditions, and Christian symbols, putting them in an interpersonal and emotional context. He gives new and interesting perspectives on many well-known bits of the Christian story.

This series has a second "special." It is by laymen and for the laity. It is not the clergy again telling the story. Lay people are telling the story. I have used "laymen" advisedly. It is men telling the story. In my experience as a pastor it has been easy to involve men in the property and finance matters of church life. It has been difficult to get them to "tell the story." This series accomplishes that purpose. Where it has been used it has been found to develop a new sense of "camaraderie in the faith" by a group of men. Is this not a definition of the church? It can be fairly said that this series takes scripture and tradition and through them builds the church.

Robert K. Nace
Forty years a Parish Pastor
Supervisor of Parish Clinical Pastoral Education
One time Moderator of the United Church of Christ

AUTHOR'S PREFACE

The genesis of the book grew out of the perennial frustration of needing to develop a meaningful Lenten experience for my parish.

With Wednesday evening worship services seemingly having taken their course, I hit upon the idea of using a secular popular talk show motif as a means of conveying the story of the lives of the Apostles, as well as the events of the final week of our Lord's life.

The book has been written in such a way as to provide any pastor a ready handbook for its implementation with a variety of settings. It can be used as a ''sermon series'' on either Sunday mornings or mid-week services, or it can be used as a program for special events during the existing calendar of a parish, such as a men's or women's breakfast or meetings. It might also be used as an easy educational tool for confirmation instruction in dealing with the Apostles.

Irrespective of the educational value derived from the information contained, the format provides a marvelous opportunity for the development of Christian community for those who commit themselves to participating in the presentations.

I would encourage one who finds this work helpful to allow your imagination to fly, so that you might receive as much blessing in the doing of it in your style as we have had in doing it in our corner of the kingdom.

ACKNOWLEDGEMENTS

The list of those to whom I am grateful for this publication cry out like the proverbial stones which refuse to be quiet, but among the most evident are the following:

Beyond all else I need to acknowledge, with gratitude, the many men of Calvary Church who have, through the last four years, taken upon themselves the portrayal of the Apostles with a dedication that would make any pastor proud to have them in his parish.

Beyond them I need to personally thank Dr. Fred Craddock, my teacher from afar, who has and continues to inspire me with fresh insights into the gospel story. It has been Dr. Craddock's preaching and teaching which comes through my writings in both ideas and phrasing with remarkable frequency. To delineate with specificity exactly which phrases and ideas they might be would be a Herculean task, for his influence has simply become a part of my being.

To my faithful secretary, Gloria Creig, for her many hours of typing and my friend, Paul Baumgartner, for his help in proofreading, I am grateful.

And finally, I would acknowledge, with gratitude, the three other publications which provided background information for this project (1) *Twelve Who Changed The World* by David MacLennan, CSS Publishing Company, Lima, Ohio, 1976; (2) *All Of The Apostles Of The Bible* by Herbert Lockyer, Zondervan Publishing House, Grand Rapids, Michigan, 1972; and (3) a work titled *The Soliloquies For The Twelve Apostles* by Earnest K. Emurian, published by W. A. Wilde Company, Natick, Massachusetts, with rights sold to Baker Book House, 1019 Wealthy Street SE, Grand Rapids, Michigan, 1968.

ASH WEDNESDAY

Opening Service
For Lenten Season

PASTOR: We are called in our Lenten pilgrimage to worship an intimate God, for there is no greater intimacy than walking through death — another's or your own. We are called to worship a person who died very publicly without mystery, theological or otherwise.

We are called to worship him who has experienced what we experience in our dying. He died with unfinished agendas, with things he wanted to talk about and we must listen! He wanted to talk of the family he was leaving, but all he could do was turn to his friend and say "Take care of my mother."

PEOPLE: We must care.

PASTOR: He wanted to talk about the people he had dealt with all his life, and all he could do was to hang there and pray for their forgiveness.

PEOPLE: We must forgive.

PASTOR: He wanted to talk about his pain, and all he could do was to say, "I thirst."

PEOPLE: We must respond.

PASTOR: He wanted permission to die. He brought it up twice. He said: "It's finished" and another time he said: "I commend my spirit."

PEOPLE: We need to say it's okay.

PASTOR: He wanted to deal with the experience of dying and the feeling that even God had forsaken him. He was absolutely alone and his closest friends were out "in hiding" somewhere, and he just hung there and screamed out into the world: "Why have you forsaken me?"

PEOPLE: And he died.

PASTOR: Since then, it means we don't have to die like that.

PEOPLE: We need to thank him.

INVOCATION (In Unison): Eternal and ever present God, you are high and mighty, yet very near and dear to those who need you most. We are bold to come before your throne of grace, and petition your benediction to rest upon us as we enter this time of penitence. Remind us that, like your Son, we face the times of our own Gethsemane, yet our days of trial may be lightened through faith in you. Remind us as well, that before we reach up to you, you are already reaching down to us, to comfort, direct, and sustain us through this our earthly pilgrimage. Our thanks to you for that assurance that leads us finally to the resurrection, himself, Jesus, our Christ.

INTRODUCTORY SERMON

Scripture: John 18:11-28

Have you ever noticed how in the examination of Scripture, you come across passages that are hard to understand? You read and read and the meaning still seems to evade. For instance, when Job is already at the end of his rope, to have his wife tell him to "curse God and die;" to have a grape farmer pay those who worked all day the same wages as those who worked an hour. Some passages are just hard to understand. Then there are some passages that one reads and it's

16

hard to believe. An axe head floating; a wheel up in the air. A body that already stinks comes out of the tomb. Some Scripture is just hard to believe.

Then there are some pages of Scripture that we plain don't like. The passage of Scripture which is ours tonight is one of those I don't like. It's the question to Peter that bothers me. "Aren't you also one of this man's disciples?" Now, I confess I used to like this passage. I loved to preach on it. I'd climb on Old Peter's back and ride him down glory road. I mean a trusted apostle! Lived with our Lord for three years. Then when it came time to pay up, what does he do but turn tail and deny, not once, but three times. Oh, I loved to point my finger and tsk, tsk my way in and out of that passage. It was great. But now I'm a little older, a little closer to the dirt myself, and like Mark Twain, I have discovered: "It's not the passages I don't understand that bother me; it's the ones I do." The longer I live and the more aware I have become of how many of my Christian brothers and sisters live, I'm confronted with some incredible contrasts. I hear people say I have a great faith and could never be brainwashed or shaken from it, and I rather subscribe to that myself, but then I am aware that I've never had to go to city hall and register the fact that I was a Christian. I'm aware that I've never been thrown into a dungeon where the sun doesn't shine, because of my belief in him. I never had a life-threatening experience because I have a lapel button that says I belong to the kingdom of God movement.

The reason I don't like that passage is that the question to Peter, "Aren't you also one of this man's disciples?" convicts me. It convicts me because I realize I have never really had a serious test to my faith. It convicts me because I know, in the secret corners of my heart, I would rather be a live coward than a dead hero. Now that I understand. How about you? Had any tests lately? If not, do we have the right to say we have faith that will stand up against every challenge?

In our church we have a Statement of Faith. One of its phrases says: "He calls us into his church to accept the cost and the joy of discipleship." In a day when we put a price tag on everything, I guess it's appropriate to ask: Well, what does it cost? It's hardly relevant to talk about the giving of our life because very few if any of us will ever be asked to do that for our faith. So, is the question relevant? Is there another way?

There must be a way for such as us to be found worthy, and there is. There is always a way. Let me illustrate what I mean.

When I was in seminary, a man by the name of Dr. Reginold Helfrich, head of Church World Service, paid a visit to our campus. While there, he told of one of his recent experiences. He had been out in Milwaukee, Wisconsin, telling the story of Church World Service and its need. After the sermon a man came up to him and asked, "What can I do to help?"

Dr. Helfrich said, "Well, the Phoenicians invented money."

The man said, "No, that's too easy. I could write a check for $5,000 and never miss it. What can I do?

Dr. Helfrich said, "What do you do?"

He said, "I own a string of restaurants."

Dr. Helfrich said, "Do you cook?"

He said, "I used to."

Dr. Helfrich said, "Then I'll tell you what to do. I want you to fly to Lambarene, Africa, to the hospital founded by Dr. Albert Schweitzer. There you will find a little Swiss cook who has not had a vacation in five years. Put her on a plane and cook for her for a month."

And he did. Anybody here doubt that he found both a cost and a joy of discipleship? The old gospel hymn says it, "Give of your best to the Master." Take whatever we have that is good enough; just give it, trusting in the paradox of our faith that says you have to give to get.

One more story, this one out of ancient history. It happened when Cyrus was king of Persia. They were in a conflict and the opposing army's general was captured and, along with his family, brought before the great king Cyrus for trial.

18

There, standing before the king, Cagular started pleading for his life.

The king said, "If I spare your life, what will you do for me?"

Cagular said, "If you spare my life, I'll be your general and make conquests in your name."

The king persisted, "And if I spare the life of your children, what will you do for me?"

He said, "If you spare the life of my children, I'll be your slave for life."

The king then asked, "If I spare the life of your wife, what will you do for me?"

He said, "If you spare the life of my wife, I'll die for you."

Well, his life was spared and, in fact, he did become a Persian General and did make conquests in the name of Cyrus.

After the trial, as they were leaving the palace, Cagular looked at his wife and said, "Did you ever see such magnificence as that room?"

She said, "I didn't notice."

He said, "Well, you must have noticed the tapestries — beautiful!"

She said, "Sorry, I missed them."

He said, "You certainly saw the king's throne, carved out of ivory — incredible!"

"Didn't see that either," she said.

Cagular, now in desperation asked, "Good heavens, woman, what did you see?"

She said, "I saw only the face of a man who said he would die for me."

Have you looked into the face of him who has died for you? Aren't you also one of this man's disciples?

Andrew
Bartholomew
James the Less

PASTOR: I can see from my vantage point in the chancel that our guests have arrived. Welcome, gentlemen, won't you please come in? *(The apostles enter and informally greet the parishioners on their way to the chancel area where there are three chairs.)* Andrew, may I begin with you? What about the feeding of the 5,000? You were the one who introduced the lad with a lunch of five loaves and two fish, weren't you?

ANDREW: Let me tell you, it was an incredible day. The Lord had been preaching and everybody lost track of time. As great as he was, and he was a real spellbinder of a preacher, eventually people were aware of their hunger. People were talking. Some wanted to leave and go home; others wanted to go down to the lake and fish; still others just wanted to feed on the words of Jesus. Well, anyway, here was this little boy with a packed lunch who said he was willing to share what he had.

I brought him to the Lord who blessed not only the boy but the food. I'll tell you the truth, to this day I don't know where all that food came from; it just seemed to appear. I've thought a lot about it since, and although I have no doubt that Jesus could have multiplied those fish and loaves, I have the feeling what really happened was that, using the example of that little boy, the Lord was able to melt the selfish hearts of all those people and everyone there shared what they had. Jesus was always having that kind of effect on people. He always brought out their best. And if you think about it, isn't that the greatest miracle of all? To melt the hardened hearts of people?

PASTOR: That's interesting. Before we leave, are you aware of the amusing story that says the reason the Scottish people chose you for their patron saint is that you "borrowed a free lunch" for the Master?

ANDREW: Oh I know, but a much more reliable reason is that it is said St. Regulus in the fifth century carried my bones to a place he called St. Andrews. I understand there was a strange and baffling game that originated at that spot. What's it called? Golf?

PASTOR: That's right, as a matter of fact there may be some correlation between its invention and scarcity of saints in the church since that time. Anyway, let me move on to your colleagues here.

Bartholomew, it has been said that "No finer tribute could be paid by one man to another than the tribute paid Queen Victoria's prime minister, William Gladstone, by John Morley when he said: 'He was one of that high and favored household who lived from a great depth of being.' " As the apostle, whom I am convinced should be called Nathanial Bartholomew, I am also convinced you must have lived from a great depth of being also. It was Philip who introduced you to Jesus. Is that right?

BARTHOLOMEW: Exactly. I'll never forget how he came to me that day and said, "We have found him of whom Moses and the prophets wrote, Jesus of Nazareth." I said, "Nazareth? Nazareth? Can anything good come out of Nazareth?" Philip said to me, "Come and see for yourself." So I started over to where Jesus was. You could have blown me over with a feather. His eyes were so penetrating. He looked at me and said, "Behold an Israelite indeed, in whom there is no guile!" You can imagine how I felt. When I gained my composure, I asked, "How did you know me?" Jesus said, "When you were under the fig tree, I saw you." It was amazing. I don't know if you are aware of it or not, but back then the fig tree was seen as a kind of private room. A fig tree grows to about 15 feet high and 25 feet wide and it acted as a little sanctuary. I used that as a special spot of prayer and meditation, so Jesus was saying in effect: "Bartholomew, I saw into the secret places of your heart, and I know the seeking that is there." I felt like quoting Psalm 139: "O Lord, thou hast searched me and known me . . . thou discernest my thoughts from afar."

PASTOR: Bartholomew, how lucky you are to have that assurance. He knew you through and through and loved you still and all.

Of course our friend James here was certainly known by our Lord as well. Being Jesus' brother, it would be easy to know and be known.

JAMES: I'm sorry, but you have me confused with another James. I can understand because there were four of us that were very close to Jesus. There was James, the son of Zebedee, and John's brother. It was that James that was martyred at 44 years of age. He was second after Stephen to have met that fate.

There was James, son of Mary and brother of Jesus, but he became a believer only after Jesus' resurrection. It must have been hard knowing his own brother didn't understand what he was doing. There was James, the father of Judas, who was neither the Iscariot nor the near relative of Jesus. And then there was me. Everything you know about me is from oral tradition. The Bible has listed only my name. Mark calls me James the Less, but he should have made it more specific and called me James the Little, for I share a distinction with Zacchaeus.

PASTOR: Well, James, we may not know a lot about what you did, but I can assure you that you are still an inspiration to all of us who may not have a lot of fame, but still try to be faithful to our calling as Christians. I have the feeling that our Master's "Well done," which will be heard at the judgment seat, will be for the known as well as the unknown. Well, all of this has been very interesting. Can you explain to us your Christian symbol?

ANDREW: Oh yes, well, I was quite a traveler. In fact, the Byzantine Church, in what is now Russia, considers me their founder. God gave me great gifts as a Preacher and Healer. But as is sometimes the case, those with gifts are those who are feared as well.

In the year 60 A.D. I was instrumental in converting the wife of Governor Aegeatis at Patrus, Greece. He was so jealous he ordered my crucifixion on a quarter cross. They tied me there and let me hang, where two days later, I died, but not before I could still preach, even from the Cross, concerning my love for Jesus.

BARTHOLOMEW: As with Andrew, my symbol also refers to my martyrdom. I won King Plymus of Armenia to Christianity. However, the brother of the king was so angry, that he had me killed. Although, I could die only once for my Lord, he used three methods. He had me flogged, crucified and beheaded. Consequently, the reference to the three knives of death.

JAMES: In the year 865, the Bishop of Iria in Spain was guided by a star to the spot of my burial. It led to Santiago, Spain. However, my recollection is that after preaching in Spain, I returned to Jerusalem and became bishop of the whole church there. I was 96 at the time so my memory is a little fuzzy, but I'm told I was thrown out of the temple by the Pharisees, and they had me stoned. I was knocked unconscious, but tradition says somebody stepped forward and finished the job with a fuller's club. I guess that's why my symbol has a club on it.

PASTOR: I really can't thank you all enough for coming, but before you have to go, do you have any questions for us?

JAMES: I would like to remind you that God's plans are not always open and obvious. Did you know that a group of German Christians were hiding Jews in the crypt of the Cathedral at Cologne during World War II? While vacationing there, the Jews carved in the stone, "We believe in God though he be silent: we believe in the light though it be dark." So I would ask: when God seems to be hidden, can you still be faithful as I was?

BARTHOLOMEW: I would ask you, "Do you have a fig tree? Do you have that special place of prayer and meditation to which you can retire and be with God?" If not, may I encourage you to do so. Now, at the beginning of Lent, is a perfect time to start.

ANDREW: If any of you are living in the shadow of an older brother or sister who has excelled, you can understand how it was to be Simon Peter's brother. I sometimes thought Mom liked him better, but I really know different. My question is: Do you feel you are among those who never make the spotlight? Are you not reckoned among the leaders of your social circle, professional or church? My question is, "Can you be content to play a secondary role in God's kingdom, knowing there is nothing we ever offer that he cannot use?"

PASTOR: Gentlemen, you have truly started our Lenten pilgrimage in a most significant way. We thank you and are looking forward to your returning to us to share the Passover. Thank you again and godspeed.

Simon the Zealot
Matthew
Thaddaeus

PASTOR: Since our visit last week from Andrew, Bartholomew and James, son of Alphaeus, I've been most eager to meet some more of our Lord's apostles. Tonight we have invited Simon the Zealot, Matthew, and Thaddaeus. Gentlemen, since I have not met you personally, may I ask you to identify yourselves?

MATTHEW: Oh, let me just make the introductions. I'm Matthew; this is Simon and this is Thaddaeus.

PASTOR: First of all let me thank you for coming and relieve my own impatience by getting right into the interview. Simon, I heard a story once of a New England town council member who at one evening meeting had to excuse himself. On his way out the door he said to the remaining members, "If anything significant comes up, I vote 'no'." St. Luke is the one who calls you Simon the Zealot, and, in our day, to be one filled with zeal is to be admired. But as I read about what you and your party were really like, it sounds to me as though you also did a lot of voting "no" on what were considered rather progressive ideas.

SIMON: Now wait a minute, it's just like you guys from the left wing press to try to tar our honor with the stick of your liberalism. Let me tell you what we're about. I had a sticker on my chariot that said: "Love it or leave it." What I meant by that was:

Love the tradition of our Father Abraham
and our law-giver Moses:
Love the kingdom that had been established;
Love the independence of Israel;
Love the memory of our beloved example,
Judas Maccabaeus, who did stand up against
those Roman imperialist dogs. He saved
Jerusalem for us and gave us access to
our temple.

You bet I loved it, and as far as I was concerned, anybody who didn't, or couldn't, may as well leave.

MATTHEW: Now, Simon, this is the 20th century, and there's little point in going and digging all that up again.

SIMON ZEALOT: Easy for you to say, you turncoat tax collector you. You fueled the coffers of the very government that had their heel on our head.

THADDAEUS: Fellows, fellows, name-calling is not the way of Christ.

SIMON: You're right, Matthew, I'm sorry, but you know how strongly I felt about that issue.

PASTOR: Matthew, what about the business of tax collecting for Rome?

MATTHEW: It's true, every word of it. But the word I want you to hear is was. He was a tax collector. If the Master can call me, he can call anybody. I was one hard cookie. Just imagine what a thick skin I had to develop. What you just heard from Simon was mild compared to the scorn heaped upon my head from even the most casual passerby.

I guess I was living proof that Jesus came to save sinners, not those who had no need of salvation. I think it was Cyprium, who years after my death, said that: "The church must be a haven for sinners and not a show place for the saints."

Anyway, I'll never forget that call. It was so simple. Just, "Follow me" and I got up and went. I'll never know what it was, except a miracle. From that day on, my life was changed. All the things I had previously counted on, like money and position and power, were of no importance. In short, for me, life was redefined.

PASTOR: What a beautiful story.

MATTHEW: Oh yeah, try going home some night from work and tell your wife you just turned in your C.P.A. license right in the middle of tax time to follow an itinerant preacher for the next three years.

THADDAEUS: You never told us, what did happen?

MATTHEW: You mean after she smelled my breath? Well, she reminded me for the millionth time how her mother always said I would never amount to anything, but then after awhile she realized what a change had taken place in my life. Though, perhaps, she never really understood, she could at least accept my decision.

SIMON: Judas, let's get off this subject, okay?

PASTOR: Thaddaeus, he called you Judas, Aren't you offended?

THADDAEUS: Not at all, for you see Judas was one of my names. I know this must be confusing for you, but it was very common in those days to have more than one name. In fact, until the 11th century of your calendar, most of the world didn't have a last name, so further words were used to identify whom one was talking about. For instance, as you know, there was another Judas in our group. So I was sometimes referred to as Judas, not of Iscariot. You must also understand, back then, names meant something.

Judas came from the Hebrew word Judah, which meant "Jehovah leads." That is how some referred to me. My friend John, who later wrote one of the gospels, made sure he always distinguished me from the traitor, from Iscariot.

Matthew here, never referred to me as Judas at all, but as Thaddaeus or Lebbaeus. Thad, in Hebrew, refers to a woman's breast and Lebbaeus, in Greek, means breast-child. I guess these were just words of endearment for me as one of the youngest of the apostles.

PASTOR: Thank you, Thaddaeus, that helps because we really don't know a lot about you.

THADDAEUS: I can understand that. I am mentioned only in passing as the one who asked a question of Jesus. I said: "Lord, how is it that you will manifest yourself to us, and not the world?" As was so often the case, it was not so much an explanation of the method, as a glorious promise. Remember, it was right after that question that he told us of the comforter that our Father would send to those who loved him. He went on to say: "Peace I leave with you: my peace I give to you . . . Let not your heart be troubled, neither let it be afraid." After that you don't have a lot of questions.

PASTOR: Thank you, Thaddaeus, that's all been very helpful, but I didn't hear anything that would explain your Christian symbol. Can you shed some light on that?

THADDAEUS: Sure. You know Jesus sent us out two by two, and if my memory serves me, Simon and I were doing a lot of mission work together. One time, however, I was sent to far-away Armenia where I was martyred. The ship with the cross as its mast simply refers to my missionary journeys.

SIMON: My Christian symbol goes right along with that: the fish and book refer to my success as a fisher of men using the gospel as my source. Sometimes either a battle axe or saw appears as well, telling of my death. I was either sawed in two or beheaded. It doesn't really matter. What matters is the truth that our Master broke all bonds of death and opened the gates to life eternal.

PASTOR: How about you, Matthew, tell us about your Christian symbol.

MATTHEW: As you know I was involved in tax collecting before Jesus called me. The marvelous thing is, God can turn any of our talents into useful means for his kingdom. I don't mind at all being remembered for what I was. It was because I was a Jew that I could later write my gospel in Hebrew to my fellow Jews. The other gospels were written in Greek. To me the Christ of history was the Christ of prophecy. Sometimes there is a battle axe pictured as well, as a reminder of my being beheaded in Ethiopia. But again, how I died and where my mortal remains were finally laid to rest is of little matter. What I want you to remember is the transformation of my life after I met Jesus.

PASTOR: Well, once again I must thank you for your visit. Before you leave, do any of you have anything to say to us?

SIMON: Yes, I do. With so much animosity in this world over so many issues, can you all remember how, even as a zealot and super patriot for Israel, Matthew, a tax collector, and I could still be united as one in Christ? My question is, "Can you do the same with those whom you perceive to be of opposite positions?"

MATTHEW: I would echo what Simon has just said, but go one step further and ask you to imagine what it would mean for you to take into your organization, or trusted circle of friends, your most despised enemy.

I remember one time, when a paralytic was brought to Jesus. His first act was to say, "Your sins are forgiven."

I'm here to tell you, our first act of reconciliation is forgiveness. I know. At the time I was the most despised in all of Israel, and I found acceptance. That good news is available to all of us.

THADDAEUS: While I was following Jesus, I often thought of the story of creation and how God made the sun to shine by day and the moon to rule the night. I also remembered that he made lots of stars as well. Together, the stars can put on a marvelous display of beauty. I was never one of the big shining major lights, but you never felt my importance was diminished. I would ask you to remember that if some time you feel as one left out, or not in the center stage.

PASTOR: It is so very humbling to be in the presence of those who walked so closely with the Master. At the same time, it's been reassuring to know that all of you found very similar life issues as we do, so our comfort level increases as well.

May I bid you farewell with an invitation to return and celebrate the Passover with us.

Philip
Thomas

PASTOR: Philip, as some of your other colleagues have visited us, we have discussed the meaning of their names. We also were able to see how many of the apostles had more than one name; they had their old name, but were given a new, or Christian, name. That doesn't seem to be the case with you.

PHILIP: That's right. I'm the only one of the apostles with a Greek name that was not changed. Philip means "love of horses." I can't say that it was prophetic in any way, unless, of course, you would associate horses with travel. I am remembered as the first foreign missionary for Christ. In fact, I'm the one who went out and found one of the apostles for our Lord. I found Bartholomew. By the same token Andrew and Peter, my friends, were of tremendous help in my associations with Jesus. We were from the same hometown, and Andrew was sort of my mentor all through our three years at the foot of Jesus.

PASTOR: If you don't mind my saying so, Philip, as I read the New Testament, you needed a mentor.

THOMAS: That's a bum rap, just like a lot of what the press has done to me.

PHILIP: Now wait a minute, Thomas, I can speak for myself. Let me ask you, just what did you read that gave you that impression?

PASTOR: Well, for instance, at the place of the feeding of the five thousand, you were the only one who was all-fired concerned about where the bread was going to come from. You calculated you had only enough money in the kitty to buy 200 penny weight of bread. It seems to me that you shouldn't have had any doubt that Jesus would have been able to handle the situation.

PHILIP: Okay, you're right. You'll probably bring up the fact that on that last night he was with us, I was the one who asked him to "show us the Father." I could cut my tongue out for asking that question. It's just that it was all happening so fast. I admit I wasn't the brightest of the apostles. In fact, I may have been a little dull, but may I remind you that my name is one of the ones that John of Patmos records in his book of Revelation, as one of the twelve cornerstones of the Holy City.

PASTOR: I agree and perhaps from a 2,000 year's perspective, my original question was a bit impertinent.

THOMAS: I'm glad to hear you say that because I'm a bit sensitive on this issue as well. I know all too well some of the things that have been written about me. I know I've been blamed for my doubting.
One writer said of me, "If ever a somber dismal note was to be struck, you could depend on Thomas to strike it." But I want to speak for Philip here, too. I've heard people in your day say "seeing is believing." But I want to remind you that "believing is seeing," and that's tougher to trust. Let's look at the end results. Both of us end up as believers.

PHILIP: Right. I believe it was Francis Bacon who said: "He who begins with certainty will end in doubt, but he who begins with doubt and pursues it faithfully, will surely end in certainty."

PASTOR: That sounds a little bit like Tennyson who said: "There lives more faith in honest doubt, than in all the creeds."

Well, I'm getting the feeling it really is a little dangerous to draw too many judgments about what was going on from this distance. So help us to understand, Thomas. What was going on in your head when you said: "Unless I place my hands in his side, I won't believe."

THOMAS: Let me put that into perspective for you. Imagine having invested yourself completely in a cause and committed yourself totally to that person who espoused that cause. Then imagine having that person taken away from you by death. Your friends then come to you and say, "We have seen your friend and he is back with us." What would you say? I know very well what you'd say. Here in Pennsylvania Dutch country you'd say, "Git ott." Right?

PASTOR: Well, maybe so, but what about before he died? When, at the last supper, you asked Jesus: "Lord, we don't know where you are going, and who will show us the way?"

PHILIP: Let me jump in here and say something. I understood that question completely. At that point we were all feeling like children sitting on the floor watching our mom and dad put on their coats on a Saturday night. Our questions were the same: "Where are you going?" "Can we come along?" And "Who's going to stay with us?"

THOMAS: Good, Philip, that's exactly how I felt. It's just that you can't look at only one side of the coin. You talk about Philip's being a bit slow minded, but are you remembering he was one of the ones to whom was given the gift of tongues at Pentecost?

PHILIP: Just imagine that I, of all people, all of a sudden was able to speak a foreign language, to tell the good news of Jesus Christ. How long would it take you to learn Pennsylvania Dutch or Russian or Chinese? I had the gift instantly. Now, when you experience something like that, you treat the gift with respect. As I've said before, I may not be the brightest, but I remember that when all the rest of us were afraid to go to Bethany with Jesus — when he heard his friend Lazarus was ill; it was Thomas here who said: "He would go so he could even die with his Lord," and he did go. I want you to remember things like that, too. I sometimes get the feeling that too many of us want only to remember the bad things about someone. It seems you have to mess up only once and it wipes out all the good that you ever did. That's pretty unfair.

THOMAS: That's only particularly true. Take our friend Peter for instance; here was a man who also at one point said he would die with our Lord rather than ever deny him, yet we all know he did deny him, not once but three times. I doubted once and will forever after be known as doubting Thomas. I don't hear anybody labeling Peter "Denying Peter." Maybe it has to do with the personality involved. In fact, I've always felt a little hurt that the gospel that I wrote was never taken more seriously.

PASTOR: I can understand that. There are some people you just like to dislike. Richard Nixon opened the door to China after 25 years of closed-door policy, but he'll always be remembered most for his stonewalling the "Watergate" issue. Anyway, it's been helpful to remember that point you made, Thomas.

Thomas, let me move to another point. You have also been referred to as "the twin." In fact the Greek equivalent of your name is Didymus, which means twin. However, in all of Scripture I've not been able to find anything that would substantiate that fact, so I'd rather doubt the story.

THOMAS: What did you say? You doubt? Well, well, all of a sudden the "folks" are as good as the "people." We have someone who may have experienced the very thing we are talking about. I think I'll just let you wonder about that. On second thought, I do have something else to say. Haven't you

36

ever felt that you were a twin? Not in the biological sense but in a psychological way. I mean the dual nature of humankind is nothing new. The one who followed us and tried so much to further the cause of Christ understood this well. Paul of Tarsus said: "The good I would do not, the evil I abhor is the very thing I would do." Maybe all of us should take a lesson from that and be a bit more tolerant of the twin in us all.

THOMAS: I didn't mean it to be a put-down, just a point to remember.

PASTOR: And a good point it is.
Well, tell us a little about your lives after the resurrection.

PHILIP: Okay, but understand we will be speaking from legendary accounts. There was just nothing written about with any great degree of accuracy.

THOMAS: Traditionally, it is believed that in a night vision, Jesus directed me to move to the east. I did, where I met and converted the original three kings who had come to pay homage at the stable. I stayed there and worked with the Zoroastreans. I was in prayer one day near what is now Bombay, when I was impaled with a lance. You can see that in my Christian symbol. I had converted Queen Tertia, an act which was not accepted well by King Midsai. The carpenter's square refers to the assumption that I did a lot of the work on the church building myself.

PHILIP: When we were talking before about how one can be remembered for one remark, my Christian symbol is a prime example. These two loaves of bread refer to my question "How shall we buy bread for all these people?"
And the cross refers either to my crucifixion or my carrying the message of the cross to so many places. You can just sort of take your choice.

37

PASTOR: Well, before you leave, do either of you have anything else you would like to say?

THOMAS: Well, yes I do, I would just like to ask if you modern day Christians feel you are any better at reserving your judgment of someone until you hear the whole story than you were in the beginning? I have worn the label "Doubting Thomas" for 2,000 years, and I can tell you that labels of any kind are hurtful and destructive. I would just ask you to learn the whole story before you make your judgment.

PHILIP: I would ask you to do the same thing, but also remind you that no matter what label the world puts on you, coming into a relationship with Jesus can change it all. Never hesitate to offer whatever it is you have to the Master. I may have been dull when he found me, but I felt like a shiny gold piece when he used me.

PASTOR: Both of you have certainly demonstrated how destructive labels and judgments can be. I know I can't undo what the centuries have done to both of you, but may I assure you of how welcome you would both be at our Passover meal. I truly hope you will be with us. Until then, thank you and God bless you.

James,
John

PASTOR: Our guests have arrived, and I would ask that you welcome them and make them feel at home with Christians of the twentieth century. What a unique opportunity to have brothers to talk to! We've talked to Andrew and we will be talking to Peter, but the two of you are a bit different. Whenever the inner circle of the disciples of Jesus is mentioned, the two of you are listed together. So we welcome this chance.

However, I also have to say that we have been told far more about you, John, than you, James. In fact, we have a lot of your own words to guide us with your gospel and other writings, John. All of that has been very helpful. We also know more about your parents than perhaps any of the other apostles, so I was wondering if you might be willing to give us some insight into home life during the first century.

JOHN: I'm certainly willing, but I think I'll yield to age and let James speak.

JAMES: Older, yes, but not necessarily wiser. My brother certainly did bring honor to our family with the gift of his wonderful pen, but sure, I'll be glad to answer your questions if I can.

PASTOR: We know your father was Zebedee, and your mother's name was Salome, but it seems after Jesus called you from mending your nets, we don't hear much about your father. Why?

JAMES: Let me say very quickly, our father was a truly good man. He was an orthodox Jew who was a very successful business man. As a matter of fact, the record says he was also there mending nets with us. He didn't have to do that; he had servants and us sons to take care of that, but his hands on attention to detail, I'm sure, contributed to his success. But sadly, he simply did not share our faith and our belief in in Jesus.

PASTOR: Did you ever think of being anything other than a fisherman?

JAMES: No, really it was the custom of the day to follow in your father's footsteps, much more than now. That's why Jesus was a carpenter, I'm sure.

PASTOR: You mean because Joseph was a carpenter?

JAMES: Exactly.

JOHN: If I can break in here, as James says. Father was a good man and it was very hard to leave him and the business, especially for James, being the older one. I've always somehow thought, though, that Jesus had Father Zebedee in mind when he said: "He who loves son or daughter more than me is not worthy of me." I must also say it was very reassuring to hear him later say to us: "Those who leave mother and father for my sake will receive a hundredfold and eternal life."

PASTOR: Tell me about your mother.

JAMES: You're up, do you want to continue?

JOHN: No, really, you go ahead.

JAMES: Well, mother was different from father in that she believed in the lordship of Jesus as soon as we did. You must also understand mother and Mary, Jesus' mother, were very close. So Jesus was known to her since his childhood. In that connection I think mother has always gotten sort of a raw deal from history. She went to Jesus with her request for John and me, so she's been called a stage door mama and over-ambitious. But just remember the relationship she had with Jesus, and then maybe it won't sound quite so presumptuous.

PASTOR: Thank you. This has been very interesting, but let me ask you a personal question. "Why did you follow?"

JAMES: When I heard Jesus use the words "I will make you into . . ." I just knew there was something lacking in my life and he held a promise to be different.

I found out what that was. You may remember Jesus nicknamed us the Sons of Thunder. Well, I'm here to tell you, he took the Niagara Falls in me and turned it into a turbine for his kingdom. He can do that, you know; take whatever you are and use it.

PASTOR: Let me ask you another personal question. Did you resent living in the shadow of John?

JOHN: Now wait a minute. I don't think he ever did. May I remind you, whenever we are listed, it's always James, the son of Zebedee, and his brother John. We had different gifts but not in an overshadowing way.

JAMES: He's right. How could I feel overshadowed when I had the privilege of being one of the inner circle, who accompanied Jesus into the chamber of death for his first victory over death, in the raising of Jairus' daughter? I was with him on the Mount of Transfiguration, and I was one of the three who went with him to the Garden of Gethsemane for prayer. Even though, I must confess, I fell asleep.

JOHN: Don't feel bad; so did Peter.

PASTOR: Speaking of Peter. When you and Peter were arrested together, James, why were you killed and not Peter?

41

JAMES: That remains a secret of him "who moved in mysterious ways his wonders to perform." All I know is, I have the distinction of being the second person named in Acts as a martyr for the faith, Stephen was the first. I will never regret the 17 years of ministry I had.

PASTOR: Seventeen years sounds like a long time, but your brother, John, not only bettered you; he outlived all of the apostles.

JOHN: That's right, I was the youngest one called and the oldest to die. What a blessing!

PASTOR: Perhaps partly because of your age and your talent, but also just because of who you were in relationship to Jesus, you have a special niche among the twelve. We have the most complete knowledge of you, even down to the fact that Ambrose, an early historial, says you were the only one of the twelve not married. Is that true?

JOHN: Yes, that's true, but that does not mean I had no family. I owned my own house, and so Jesus, understanding the pain in both his mother's heart as well as his own, made provisions for that while he was on the cross. He gave us to one another's care.

PASTOR: Why do you think you were chosen? Didn't Jesus have some brothers who could have cared for her?

JOHN: Yes, but at that point his brothers didn't believe in him yet. We say that "Blood is thicker than water," but Jesus proved "Spirit is thicker than blood."

PASTOR: James told us of your nickname being Sons of Thunder. It seems you became son of peace and love.

JOHN: How can you help it, being in the presence of perfect goodness? It's sort of like the old story of a gardener who found a piece of fragrant clay in his field and asked the clay: "What are you?" Are you a rose?" "No," answered the clay, "but they laid me near one." To lay my head on Jesus' bosom as I did took this piece of clay and transformed me.

PASTOR: Speaking of that incident — you are referred to over and over again as, "the one whom Jesus loved?" Didn't that create some jealousy among the others.

JOHN: No, as I pointed out in my writing, Jesus played no favorites. "He loved all whom he had chosen," but he found in me a kindred spirit. I think he delighted in my capacity for the mystery of spiritual truth.

PASTOR: You certainly had that. Of all the gospel writers, you simply accept Jesus' mysterious creative power better than any other. You even start your gospel with the appeal to the "Word which dwelt among us." That's pretty mysterious.

JOHN: It is until you've experienced it, and then it's as child's play.

PASTOR: John, let me move now to your Christian symbol. Can you explain the cup with a serpent coming out of it?

JOHN: As you know, none of us apostles designed our own Christian symbols, but I would imagine it refers to one of two things. Either that time when legend says they tried to poison me and the poison became a serpent, or my preference is to think it refers to that request of mother's for James and me to sit on his right and left side when he came into his kingdom. Do you remember his question in return? "Can you drink the cup, the bitter cup from which I must drink?" He was referring, of course, to his crucifixion.

PASTOR: James, how about your Christian symbol?

JAMES: Mine is a sword and a scallop. The sword refers to my martyrdom — the first of the apostles to die under Herod Agrippa I. The scallop is a symbol for my long pilgrimages.

PASTOR: It's been most enlightening to have you both with us. Do you have any last comments?

JAMES: I would just like to repeat again how fellowship with Christ can transform a person. All that which is dead within us truly can come alive again. Even those things that we think are important can be sacrificed. I know, I left more than most — good home, ready-made occupation, father of means and credibility, and a gentle loving mother. I knew the prospect of martyrdom for many years, but did not turn away. I drank the cup, the bitter cup, from which he drank, and it turned into the sweetness of life beyond measure, both here and above. Are you willing to do the same?

JOHN: As for me, I would just like to quote from me. I like how one of your modern translators puts it:

> "Dear friends, let us love one another, because love is from God. Everyone who loves is a child of God and knows God, but the unloving know nothing of God. For God is love; and his love was disclosed to us in this, that he sent his only Son into the world to bring us life . . . God is love; he who dwells in love is dwelling in God, and God in him . . . there is no room for fear in love; perfect love banishes fear."

My only question is, do you believe it?"

PASTOR: John, I for one can say, "of course I believe it." But I must also quickly confess acting on belief is far more

44

difficult. Yet without the belief as a starting point we never would act. So, thank you for your love as brothers and your love as Christians to inspire us. Speaking of love, we are expecting both of you at the table of love when we celebrate the Passover with the Lord. Until then, Shalom.

Peter, Judas

(Judas arrives late, clutching a money purse throughout.)

PASTOR: Gentlemen, thank you for coming, but let me begin by confessing to you, I'm a nervous wreck. I mean the prospects of interviewing one of the apostles who was central in the drama that unfolded during the last week of our Lord's life, in itself, is a bit intimidating. But Judas and Peter, that's really too much. So let me get to it. I know that you know that I know what both of you did and especially you, Judas. I was even worried that you might not appear with him, Peter.

PETER: What Judas did is a matter of records, and God has already judged his act. I'm not here to condemn anymore, I'm here to give testimony to the fact that there but by the grace of God go I.

PASTOR: Do you mean you could have done what he did?

PETER: Maybe not in the same way, but may I remind you that on that last night, when Jesus predicted that one of us would betray him, from the eldest to the least, we all had to question, "Am I the one?" We all had our own Achilles' heel; we all had our own vulnerability. In my case, thank God I had a chance to amend.

PASTOR: What do you mean by that?

PETER: Well, you said you knew I knew you knew, so don't play dumb. There I was, the big fisherman who cursed and lied and felt like a coward in front of that little chambermaid who was no bigger than a minute.

I was in the garden outside where they had taken Jesus and all she said was: "Aren't you also one of this man's disciples?" And not once, but three times, I denied it just like he predicted I would do.

JUDAS: Oh, dear passionate Peter. Pastor, this man couldn't give the weather report without making it sound like the second coming. Always there to both lament as well as to praise, and this went for himself as well as the rest. No one, even Jesus, was safe from his mood swings. He was the only one who dared to rebuke Jesus himself.

But getting back to that little tirade we just witnessed, a much more calculating mind like mine, reminds everyone that Peter was the only one who had the courage even to follow Jesus in the first place.

PASTOR: Speaking of your mind, Judas, I'd love to get into it for awhile and try to figure out what was really going on that led to your action of selling Jesus.

JUDAS: I'm not sure that I even know, but I'll answer if you have specific questions.

PASTOR: Okay. Throughout history there have been several theories advanced, and I'd like to explore them with you. First, some have said that you were predestined. Someone had to be chosen to do the deed so that prophecy could be fulfilled. You were the one. If it weren't you, it would have been someone else.

JUDAS: Now think about that for a minute. If you carry that to its logical conclusion, then God is the sinner since God chose me. What a cop out. I don't buy it.

PASTOR: Okay, how about this one. Money. You were just plain greedy. Certainly Jesus warned all of you of its perils.

48

He did say: "What does it profit a man to gain the whole world and lose his own soul." Yet the lure seems to be there for all of us. Maybe just a bit more for you.

JUDAS: Let me acknowledge a truism that I think does fit here. Someone has said: "Of all the winds that blow across love, there is none so destructive as money." You're right, money is a terrible evil when misused, but may I now blow your bubble. If it were only money I was after, I could have gotten more from Caiaphas. Try again.

PASTOR: A a matter of fact, I do have another theory.

JUDAS: Why doesn't that surprise me?

PASTOR: How about the fact that you were a disillusioned patriot?

JUDAS: Plausible. After all, I was a good Jew. I had heard the stories of how the Messiah was to come. I can remember sitting at the feet of my Rabbi as he would paint that word picture of the Messiah coming out of heaven on a white steed, call a messianic banquet of the 12 tribes, and re-establish the kingdom of the Jews. We would then go about overthrowing the Roman tyrants. What did we get? Not a white steed carrying a king, but a donkey carrying a carpenter. Not representatives of 12 tribes, but 12 ragtag throw-togethers; not a banquet at the temple, but bread and wine in an upper room. Let me ask you, would you be a little disappointed? I was, and some say my action was to try to force the hand of Jesus to get it back on the right track of an earthly kingdom.

PASTOR: Are they right?

JUDAS: Partially, but if you really pushed me, I'd have to say it was simply a case of the dark side of my personality dominating. We all have a shadow side and mine overtook good. That was really nothing new. Amos describes those selling "the righteous for silver and the poor for a pair of shoes." Even today, how do you reconcile your big business religions where it is hawked just as in our day? Maybe if Jesus were here, he'd cleanse some of your temples. And how about you, Pastor? Do you ever think about those words used at yours and others' ordination? The presiding bishop stands and says, "Having examined this candidate and found him worthy of the high calling of Christ?" We were, and are, all called by Grace, not works.

PASTOR: As a sheep before the shearer is dumb, I stand silent.

PETER: Don't let him do that, Pastor, he's getting off the point. He's diverting your attention away from himself.

PASTOR: Whatever he did I'm not about to go back for awhile. Let me talk to you, Simon Bar Jona, as you were first known.

PETER: Simon Bar Jona just means Simon, son of Jona. If I had been English, my name would have been Simon Johnson, but I much prefer the title given me by Jesus — Petros, meaning Rock. You translate that as Peter.

PASTOR: We really do know a lot about you. You're named more than any other apostle. As I read the accounts, I think you must have had some assertiveness training. You spoke on nearly every occasion. It seems you had a rule that said, "When in doubt, speak."

PETER: Maybe you're right, but let me also remind you that Jesus corrected me more than any other, too.

PASTOR: Peter, there are so many incidents in your life. I want to know about. Let me just start to ask about them, okay? First, tell us about Pentecost.

PETER: It was terrific. Just imagine, there we were, all gathered after Jesus left us, terribly confused as to what to do, when all of a sudden something happened to one of us, then another, and finally, we all felt it. All I can say is it was so comforting to know he was still with us, only in a different form. To top it off, he gave us all a gift, the gift of speaking in foreign languages, better to be able to communicate the good news of salvation. Not only that, but there was a new aliveness in our native tongue as well. Remember how John and I confounded the Council at Jerusalem? Imagine a couple of smelly fishermen speaking with eloquence. It was called charisma, which means gift. That's what it was, a gift.

PASTOR: How about your walking on water? Did you really do that?

PETER: Sometimes I think you get hung up on details and miss the real point. If I did or didn't doesn't prove anything; the real point is that when you take your eyes off Jesus as your Savior, that's when you sink.

PASTOR: Okay. How about your being the founder of the Roman Church from which modern Roman Catholicism claims its origin?

PETER: Once again, let's look at the big picture. When Jesus said: "Peter, upon this rock I will build my church," I admit my ego was very well satisfied, but I think he meant his church would be built by people with my qualities. It's a shame you are so divided on the issue of apostolic succession. The real point is, Christ can call and use anyone.

PASTOR: One more, while we still have time. Tell us about your controversy at Jerusalem you had with Paul.

PETER: Oh yes, wonderful Paul. After his conversion he was so gung-ho. If you cut him, his blood would have come out singing: "Jesus, Lover of My Soul." What a great man and how we need more like him! It's just that I felt he was a little overzealous in keeping the faith pure. He said all had to follow the same path as he and all of the rest of us did. Namely, he felt everyone had to start as a Jew with circumcision. I wanted it to be more inclusive, less exclusive. I felt baptism was the new circumcision and should be open to all — Gentiles as well as Jews.

He came around. Remember he said: "In Christ there is neither Jew nor Greek, male or female, slave or free, but all are one in Christ."

PASTOR: Let me bring Judas back into the conversation here and ask you to tell us of your Christian symbol and your death.

JUDAS: Well, it is just plain blank yellow and I guess history has decided to follow that old saying: "If you can't say anything good about someone don't say anything at all." As for my death, it's very clear. After I saw what my act was about to do, I tried to stop it. I went to the religious leaders to confess and return the money. Maybe if I had been met even then with more understanding, that dreadful night could have been saved and I would not be remembered as the "Son of Perdition." Martin Luther translated that as "Lost Child." I know that's the way I felt, so I hanged myself in Potter's Field.

PASTOR: I'll get back to you again, but in the meantime I'll ask you, Peter, to do the same for us.

PETER: My Christian symbol tells a couple things. First, there is an upside down cross. It indicates the method of my death. When they came to crucify me, I said I wasn't even worthy to die as my Lord, so they obliged me and turned me over. This happened at the hands of Nero, the Roman Emperor. It seems among my converts in Rome were many of Nero's mistresses.

Nero did a lot of fiddling around other than with his violin, so when these women became chaste, he was more than a little upset.

As for the keys, one is gold and the other silver, referring to our Lord's statement: "Peter, upon this rock I will build my church." The two colors are for both the earthly and heavenly kingdoms.

PASTOR: There's so much more about both of your lives we could talk about. I hate to see it end, but do you have any last thought for us?

JUDAS: There's no point in trying to say it in any other way but straight out. I personify the possibility of the prostitution of the soul. I have no excuses. This man Jesus didn't deserve what happened to him. Even after I kissed him to identify him to the authorities, he still called me friend. You see, divine love never retaliates.

There are a couple other things I want you to remember as well. First, understand that what you are to be, you are now becoming. Nobody becomes a saint suddenly any more than he becomes corrupt suddenly. So, never be careless in shunning little sins; they become big ones. Sin has an awful power to grow.

Finally, remember from my life that repentance can come too late. When that's the case, you can understand John's description of my end. He said, "Judas went out and it was night." It was night indeed, and in the darkness of my soul I lost it all.

PETER: If there is anything that is evident in my own life it is how Jesus taught even me humility. That's what I would like to pass on to you as well. You need not always be in charge, or fear the Master will direct you in ways not for your own good. Take the incident in my life when we had been fishing all night and not caught a thing. Then, at dawn, when everybody know the fishing was over for the night, Jesus, standing on shore, sent us out with new instructions. He told us to cast the nets on the other side. My first internal response was to question what a carpenter would know about fishing.

Secondly, I wanted to say, "But we've always done it that way, why should we change now?"

Finally, I confess I went out in the boat to do it his way, mostly out of anger, only to show him he was wrong and I knew better. Well, you know the end of the story. We had more fish than we could even haul in. That's when I knew; I really knew him to be Lord of my whole life. My challenge to you is to trust him and to adopt John's prayer: "Lord, help me to decrease that thou might increase."

PASTOR: We have received so many new insights into your lives. I want to thank you for your honesty and candor. That's not always easy and you have both done it well. Next week is the Passover and we are looking forward to seeing you again.

The Passover Seder

After a brief opening worship, the congregation is dismissed to gather at the Passover meal where an abbreviated Seder, with all the appropriate food, is served. At the beginning of the meal, Jesus and the apostles arrive with Jesus washing their feet before the meal begins. Judas arrives late, clutching a money bag. During the serving of the meal, the pastor interrupts with the reading of the Maundy Thursday narrative, which ends with the prediction of betrayal. That prediction is the only words Jesus speaks. At that prediction all of the apostles, who have been seated at a long table, strike the da Vinci pose. Each then, in turn, move to the back of Jesus to make their reflective statement and return to the pose.

After all have spoken, Judas leaves prior to the others, and the congregation is dismissed again to the sanctuary where the evening began. Upon arrival they find the Gethsemane scene with Jesus in prayer and the apostles asleep. As the Scripture continues to be read, all of the action is pantomimed, including "the kiss." The worship is then ended with the veiling of the cross.

(The order of services follows on the next two pages.)

PASSOVER SEDER/COMMUNION
WITH
THE APOSTLES

PRELUDE

HYMN

SOLO

INVITATION TO THE PASSOVER

INVOCATION

(Dismissal to the social hall for recreation of the Passover meal. The ushers will assist you.)

APOSTLES ENTRANCE   Mark 14:12-17

WASHING OF FEET   John 13:5

SERVING OF MEAL   Luke 22;15

JESUS' PREDICTION   Luke 22:15

APOSTLES RESPONSE *(speaking in this order)*
1. Andrew
2. Bartholomew
3. James the Less
4. Simon the Zealot
5. Matthew
6. Thaddaeus
7. Philip
8. Thomas
9. James
10. John
11. Judas
12. Peter

SERVICE OF HOLY COMMUNION   Matthew 26:26-29
  served by Apostles

HYMN   Matthew 26:30-32
            "Go to Dark Gethsemane"
  1. Go to dark Gethsemane,
      Ye that feel the tempter's pow'r;
    Your Redeemer's conflict see;
      Watch with him one bitter hour;
    Turn not from his griefs away;
      Learn from him to watch and pray.

        (The ushers will assist us as
        we return to the Sanctuary.)

GETHSEMANE WATCH   Matthew 26:36-45
  in Sanctuary

HYMN
  2. See him at the judgment hall,
      Beaten, bound, reviled, arraigned;
    See him meekly bearing all!
      Love to man his soul sustained.
    Shun not suffering, shame, or loss;
      Learn of Christ to bear the cross.

  3. Calvary's mournful mountain view;
      There the Lord of glory see,
    Made a sacrifice for you,
      Dying on the accursed tree.
    "It is finished!" hear his cry:
      Trust in Christ and learn to die.

JUDAS' BETRAYAL   Mark 14:43-45

HYMN

VEILING OF CROSS

BENEDICTION

POSTLUDE

INVITATION TO THE PASSOVER

The invitation to the Passover is ancient in origin and comes not from man but from God himself. It's an invitation that carries with it the hope of new life and the promise of God to be faithful in the future as he has been faithful in the past. The Passover is the celebration of man's ability to follow a God of providence and grace. It is a joyous remembrance, and stands as the cornerstone of the Christians' most central sacrament — holy communion. For it was at the Passover that Jesus told his followers of a new bread from heaven that a man may eat of and never die. It was at the Passover that his followers learned of the new pascal lamb. The lamb of God, whose blood was shed as an offering made once but of force always.

So we are invited again to come to the Passover of God. A Passover from the old to the new; from bondage to freedom; from death to life eternal.

ANDREW

I have just heard something I don't think I can believe. I heard my Lord and my Master predict that one of us was to betray him. Betray? In what way? By whom? "One of you," he said. That includes me, Andrew. I know I'm not a gifted man, and others have served with greater capacity and far more talent. But I've been faithful. I brought Peter, my own brother, to meet Jesus. I've been thrilled at the transformation in Peter's life. I was the one who found the small lad with the loaves and fishes, and I brought him to the Master's feet as well.

Right up to the present, I've always been bringing people to the Messiah, not in betrayal that would take the Master from us and others. Only recently, I brought some Greeks to Jesus who were seeking more from their lives.

So I have used the gifts that I had, limited though they were, to bring others to the source of that abundant life which he promised and which I have experienced. I know, in my heart, he is the Lamb of God, the long-awaited Messiah.

How could it be me? I am one of his disciples. Yet, I know as well, that is no protection from my own vulnerability. Could it be Andrew? Oh, dear God, is it I?

BARTHOLOMEW

Is it possible that Jesus just included me in a prediction of the unthinkable? Me? Bartholomew? Disciplined as a disciple at the feet of John the Baptist?

I was present at his first miracle at the wedding feast in Cana. I made my confession of belief early. Philip introduced me to Jesus, and the penetration of the Master to get to my very heart bade me to say right then: "Rabbi, you are the Son of God, you are the King of Israel."

Of course, I can't forget as well that when Philip first told me of having found "Him of whom Moses in the law and the prophets wrote, Jesus of Nazareth, the son of Joseph," I asked in return, "Can anything good come out of Nazareth?" How that has haunted me. I should have known. My former teacher, John the Baptist, was predicting it. Is the vulnerability of doubt, exposed by my question, coming to life again?

Oh, dear God, if only I could return to the sanctuary of my fig tree from which I was called, and there search my heart so as to know, is it I? Is it I?

JAMES THE LESS

James the Less. That's me. James the Less. I always assumed they were making reference to my size, or to my position in the order of calling. I was among those called after his public ministry had already begun. And now, a prediction of betrayal. I can't even imagine who it could be. I feel secure in my faith. I can trace my spiritual heritage through my father Alphaeus right back to Gad, one of the 12 sons of Jacob. I saw Jesus baptized. I felt the heavens open that day and sensed the proclamation of God's endorsement of His Son.

Since I accepted his call, I have never looked back.

And yet, are past deeds done, and appeal to heritage, enough to immunize me from vulnerability and my own hidden weakness? It would be an act of insanity, but there it is for all to hear. "One of you . . ." Is it I? Is it I?

SIMON THE ZEALOT

I have feared this night with all my heart. A betrayer among us. I, Simon the Zealot, swear to all, if I were to have my sword, I would put it to the throats of everyone at this table until the dog confessed. But then what? Could I, or would I finish the act of taking an eye for an eye and a tooth for a tooth? If I did, by that very act I would be revealing my own vulnerability. Have I so quickly forgotten how he said, "You have heard it said, 'An eye for an eye and a tooth for a tooth. But I say to you, do not resist one who is evil.' " The very fact that my temper has just flared as it did tells me the way of my blood-thirsty revolutionary past is not completely buried.

But I do know better. I have known since the day I laid down my sword with which I fought the earthly powers, that the kingdom of which he spoke was not of this world.

As a military man I thought I understood the unconditional surrender of myself to his love. But what I forgot was that to surrender to God's love does not imprison, but sets us free. Free to love, but also free to fail. Who is the failure? Is it I? Is it I?

MATTHEW

Am I paranoid, or did I see some eyes look in my direction when our Lord predicted what he did? Were they saying by their glance: "You can't change a leopard's spots, nor can you change a tax collector's heart?"

But I did change. He changed everything about me. He changed even my name from Levi to Matthew.

They were there in my home the night I entertained Jesus, and the Pharisees complained that he would dare associate with a publican such as I. They were also there to hear his answer: "Those who are well have no need of a physician, but those who are sick," he said. But what captivated my heart was the added words of comfort, "For I came not to call the righteous, but sinners, to repentance." I did repent and I did leave all of my past at this simple "Follow me."

Since then I have spent days studying our Scripture, not only to convince myself Jesus is the fulfillment of every prophecy of God's anointed, but to learn better the ways of writing.

The world must know of this Man's teaching, but especially the Hebrews, and I can do that. I am a Hebrew and I will record his sermon delivered on the mountain three years ago about love and the good news of God's salvation.

But now we hear bad news, terrible news, a betrayer is dipping bread with the perfect example of trust and love. Who can it be? A hated tax collector? Oh, Dear God, is it I? Is it I?

THADDAEUS

It wasn't a moment before he spoke of betrayal, that I was thinking to myself, how much this night and this meal and all of us could be compared to the 12 tribes of Israel. Just as all of the tribes have their roots in Father Israel, so Jesus called the 12 of us to become the cornerstones of his new kingdom.

Why he called me, Thaddaeus, I'll never know. The others are so much more worthy of the call, but call me he did and I have never been sorry I took on the yoke of salvation.

I was in Jerusalem when I first heard that wonderful invitation, "Come unto me, all ye that labor and are heavy-laden, and I will give you rest. Take my yoke upon you and learn of me, for I am meek and lowly in heart, and you will find rest unto your souls; for my yoke is easy and my burden is light."

But now, our Master, who has carried so many of our burdens, has one thrust upon him that is unthinkable. One of us, one of his trusted 12 will betray him. Will the blood be on all of our heads, or will it be one we least suspect? Peter, James, Philip, Thaddaeus? Thaddaeus? Is it I? Is it I?

PHILIP

Could it be that what we just heard had anything to do with my inappropriate request? How was I, Philip, limited Philip, to know? Things have happened so quickly since last Sunday when he was hailed as King. I wasn't really doubting; it's just that there has been a sense of impending doom, and I wanted to know everything I could. So I ask. It seemed an innocent enough desire. "Lord," I said, "Show us the Father, and we shall be satisfied." No sooner had the words dribbled out of my mouth and hit the floor, when I wished the floor itself would swallow me. It didn't and I had to hear him say, "Have I been with you so long, and yet you do not know me, Philip?"

Oh Lord, I do know you. I know your love and because of your love I know the Father.

What I don't know, is how anyone in his right mind could betray that love. Who could it be? Could it be Philip? Is it I? Is it I?

THOMAS

Thomas the twin. Thomas the one of dual nature. Thomas the one who demands proof before commitment.

But now I want no proof of what I have just heard. I want no collaboration of what I fear most in myself, that my very doubting nature will be my undoing.

He knows. He suspects. But how could he suspect me? When all the others fell away in fear to accompany him to Bethany when Lazarus died, I was the one who exhorted the rest to go with him even if it meant our death. For of what value would life have been without him in whom we found our life?

The time since I chose to follow him has been the best of my earthly journey. I'll never forget that sermon early in his ministry when He promised blessing for those who were persecuted for righteousness' sake. My mind's eye is alive with visions of him rebuking a stormy sea, or tenderly touching the blind or maimed.

But I know from the bitter hate that has been building because of his popularity, his prediction has great validity. No doubt about it. But who? Is it I? Is it I?

JAMES

For three years now, I have been privileged beyond all reason of merit to be among the closest of those who followed Jesus. I, James, the son of a fisherman, stand as proof of God's grace. How else could one explain his taking a "sun of thunder" and capturing his spirit as he did the restless waves on the Sea of Galilee, and now it has come to this. Now I understand his answer to mother last week, when she requested a seat in the kingdom for John and me.

63

Jesus asked us in return if we were able to drink the bitter cup or be baptized with the baptism which he was to undergo? Oh, how naive of us to answer so quickly with, "We are able."

It's difficult for any of us to hypothesize our own mortality, and so naturally I thought I was able. But tonight, tonight in the darkest corner of my soul, I confess my fear. Tonight I don't fear dying as much as I fear living, having been found to be unworthy of all the trust he has placed in me. Worst of all, I fear that in the final hour I will not be able to withstand the baptism of fire.

Is that the betrayal to which he just referred? Is it I? Is it I?

JOHN

To be chased by love, as I have been, is finally to accept the mystery of God's perfect presence right here on earth. It is not to say I understand, it is only to say I accept.

For I stand unashamedly before the world and say, "I love this Man as I have loved no other." A mystery to be accepted, for to seek an explanation would be to diminish uniqueness. To look for other examples would be to deny the grace imparted in the gift.

But betrayal? That is beyond mystery, beyond explanation. That is to confront the impossibility of rationalizing the irrational.

Betray the Man who said to Nicodemus, "For God so loved the world that he gave his only begotten Son, that whosoever believeth in him should not perish but have everlasting life." No matter what happens this night, I swear I will write that and much more of his message for all the world to know.

Yet love is sometimes blind. Am I missing something of this "Word that has come to dwell among us?" Is it out of love the betrayal is to come? Why do we hurt those we love the most? Oh, dear God, is that it? Will the source of my joy be the cause of his pain? Is it I? Is it I?

JUDAS

He knows who it is that is about to betray him, so why is he playing coy? Why not come out with it, so I could at least make one last challenge to the role of reason and practicality?

All of the things we have heard for three years about a kingdom of freedom will not come without action. Wishing it so is not enough. It takes power and money — that's what the world understands. We can not continue to tolerate the waste as in Mary's using expensive ointment to wash his or anybody else's feet. If I now have 30 pieces of silver on my person, let it be evidence to my responsibility as elected treasurer of this group. And, if he had not needed such as me, why did he choose me?

I know I have been a convenient scapegoat for all the rest to use. By pointing to my sins by my partners, the attention is diverted away from their own. But God knows, I'm not as black as they think, nor are they as white as they pretend. I hope my plan only works and then they'll thank me.

But what if it doesn't? What if he still refuses to move? What should I do? Confess, or like the others self-righteously ask, is it I? Is it I?

PETER

If I am such a big fisherman, why do I feel so small and helpless? If he sees me as a rock, why do I sense that this night my character is more like mush? If I am to be the leader of these men, why am I so hesitant to know what direction to go? If I, Peter, have an opinion on every subject, why am I now speechless on this situation? If my impetuous nature is still alive, why is my knife still in my sheath? Even if I drew it, whose heart would I pierce? Who could do this dastardly deed to this one who has given so much to all, but especially to me?

He used my boat as a pulpit to preach to the multitudes. He taught me the meaning of grace on that morning after our abundant catch of fish and I fell at his feet and said: "Depart from me, O Lord, for I am a sinful man." His answer was to give me the keys to his kingdom, here and above. Why me? My pride allowed the ordination to stand without protest, but how could I have known the burden that might come my way without his presence?

Oh, what should I do? What can any of us do? How can I go on living with this mixture of good and evil, of doubt and trust? I affirmed my loyalty to him only this evening in saying I would follow him to death. And he answered in return that even I, Peter, the rock would deny him three times before morning. What does that mean? How can that be? Am I the one? Is it I? Is it I?

PASSOVER MEAL ELEMENTS

After the brief worship service in the sanctuary, the people arrive at the tables which are already set with the elements of the Passover meal. They consist of the following:

Roasted Egg: representing the sacrificial pascal lamb.

Horseradish: to denote the bitter suffering of the Hebrews.

Charoset: representing the clay with which the Hebrews worked, (Charoset is a combination of chopped apples, nuts, and honey, with optional cinnamon for the condiment. A suggested recipe would be:

50 servings: 24 tart apples unpealed and finely chopped
6¼ cups of ground walnuts
5 cups of Passover wine
5 cups of honey
3⅛ teaspoons of ground cinnamon
Combine all and let stand one hour before serving.

Parsley: to signify the luxury of freedom, but dipped into the cup of salt water becomes a reminder that freedom was won through tears and weeping.

Wine is consumed as a reminder of the promises of freedom.

Matzo, which is the unleavened bread of the Passover, refers to the haste with which the children of Israel had to leave as well as the memory of how little it takes for a free person to stand on their own.

During the meal, the pastor asks a youth four questions from the Seder service. They are:

PASTOR: Why on this night do we eat unleavened bread?

YOUTH: The unleavened bread which we now eat is because the dough of our ancestors had not time to become leavened. They baked unleavened cakes of the dough which they had brought forth out of Egypt, for it was not leavened, and they could not tarry, neither had they made any provisions for themselves.

PASTOR: Why do we eat bitter herbs?

YOUTH: This bitter herb which we eat is because of the embittered lives of our ancestors in Egypt, as it is said: They embittered their lives with hard bondage, with all manner of labor in the field.

PASTOR: Why do we eat Charoset?

YOUTH: Our ancestors were forced to labor in mortar and brick, and all their labor was imposed upon them with rigor. We eat charoset to remember the mortar and the brick.

PASTOR: Why do we lean forward during the ceremony of the Seder?

YOUTH: Ye shall say, it is a sacrifice of the Passover unto the Lord, who passed over the houses of the children of Israel in Egypt, when he smote Egyptians, and spared our houses, and the people bowed themselves and worshiped.

Everyone then shares the meal until it is interrupted with the Scripture and Jesus speaks his prophecy of betrayal.

THE APOSTLES' SHIELDS

In this series, congregations have the opportunity to create shields, which display the coat of arms or symbols of each apostle. These shields may be displayed in the front of the church during the service pertaining to the specific apostle.

The following section contains directions to create the shields. The material used for this visual part of the worship setting can vary from felt to poster board, depending on the interest of the artist creating the shield.

Color suggestions are provided. These are based on various traditions.

ANDREW

Blue shield
Silver cross (sometimes red)

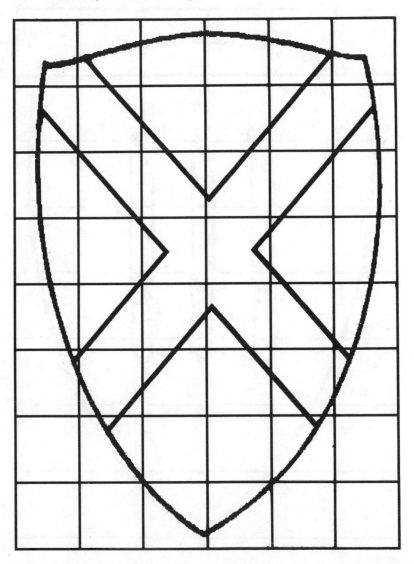

BARTHOLOMEW

Red shield
Silver knife with gold handle

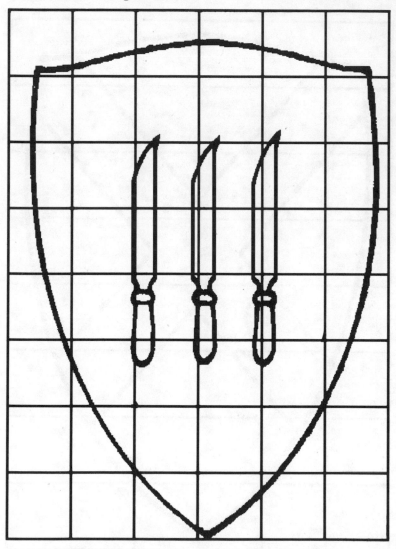

JAMES THE LESS

Red shield
Silver saw

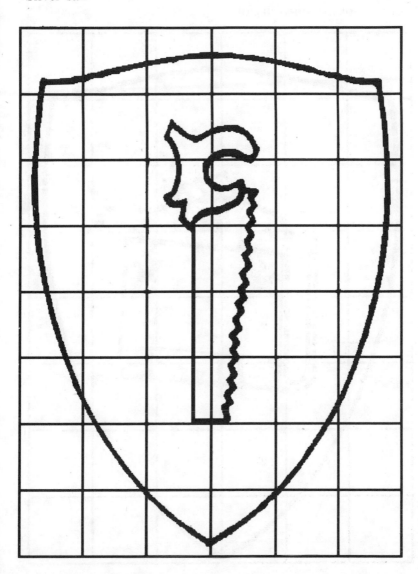

73

SIMON THE ZEALOT

Red shield
Silver fish
Buff book trimmed in gold

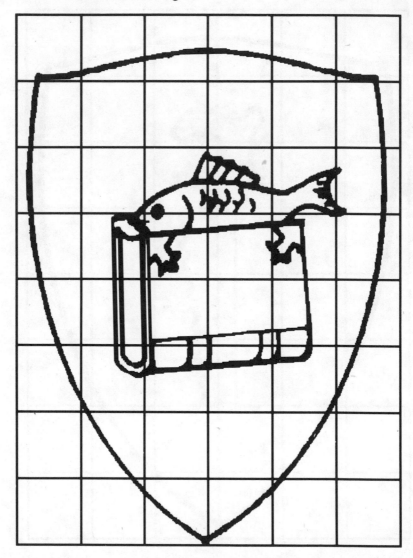

MATTHEW

White shield
Red border
Blue bags (sometimes gold)

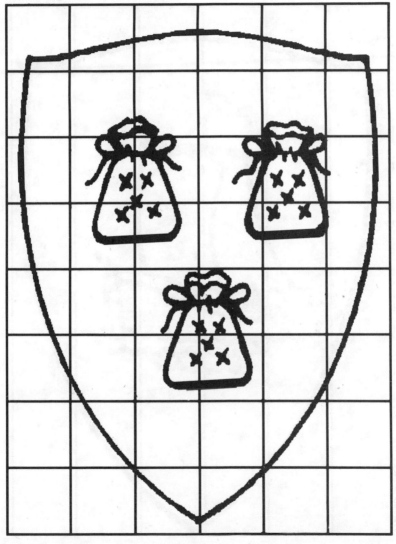

THADDAEUS

Red shield
Gold ship
Silver sails and rope

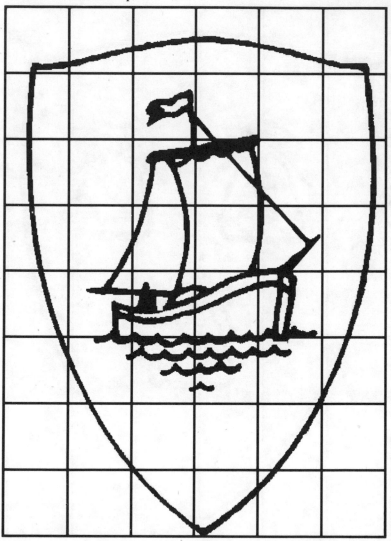

PHILIP

Red shield
Gold cross and loaves

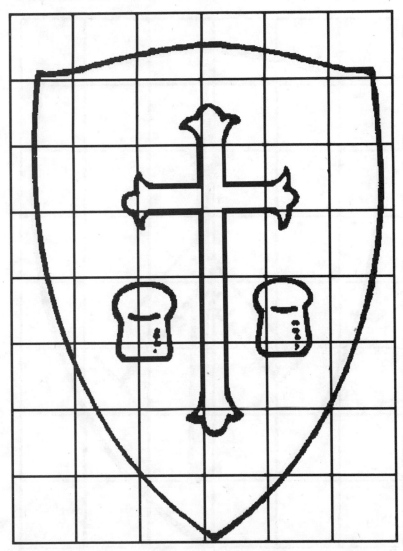

THOMAS

Blue shield
Gold spear and carpenter's square

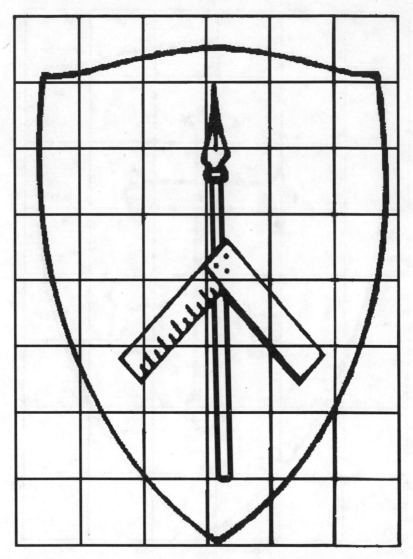

JAMES

Blue shield (sometimes red)
Gold scallops

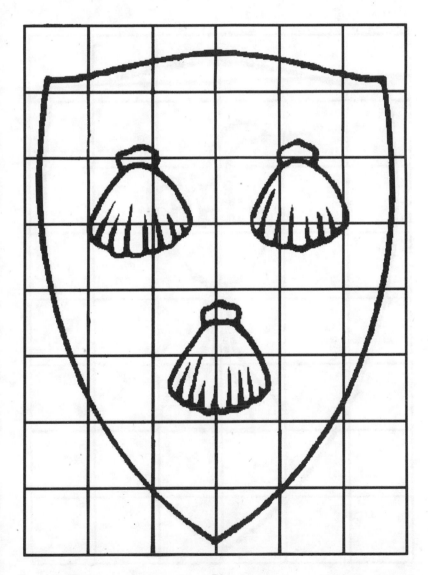

JOHN

Blue shield
Silver chalice
Red serpent

PETER

Blue shield (sometimes brilliant red)
One gold key, one silver
White cross

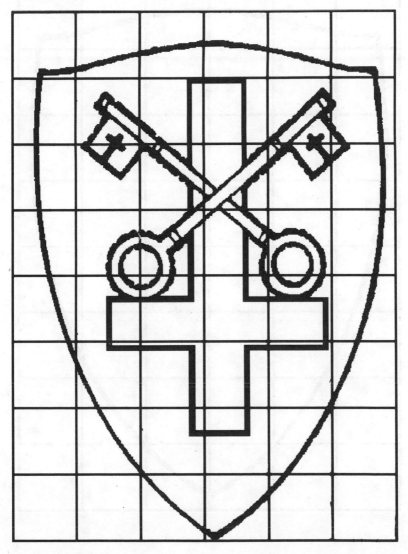

JUDAS

Yellow shield, no symbol

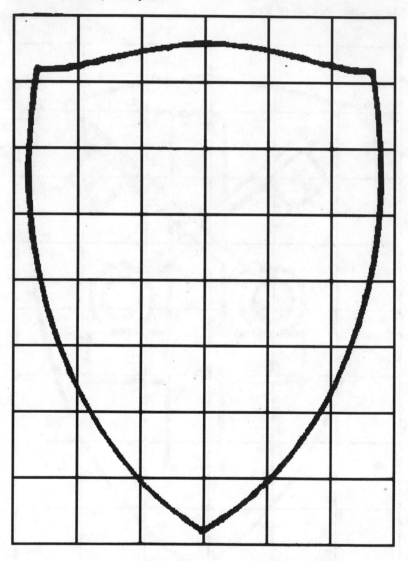

INDICES